A New True Book

MONKEYS AND APES

By Kathryn Wentzel Lumley

*This "true book" was prepared
under the direction of
Illa Podendorf,
formerly with the Laboratory School,
University of Chicago*

CHILDRENS PRESS ™

CHICAGO

Capuchin monkey

PHOTO CREDITS

Zoological Society of San Diego—2, 10 (lower left), 21 (D.K. Brockman), 22 (bottom), 27, 37 (2 photos)

Allan Roberts—4, 10 (lower right), 19, 22 (top), 25, 39, (left), 40, 43

Root Resources: ©Kenneth W. Fink, Cover, 6, 16, 31; ©Anthony Mercieca—8

James P. Rowan—35 (2 photos), 39 (right), 44

Lynn M. Stone—10 (top), 15 (2 photos), 29

R.A. Masek—12

Ray Hillstrom—32, 41

Cover—Lowland gorilla

Library of Congress Cataloging in Publication Data

Lumley, Kathryn Wentzel.
  Monkeys and apes.

  (A New true book)
  Includes index.
  Summary: Describes the physical characteristics, habits, and natural environment of monkeys and apes.
    1. Monkeys—Juvenile literature.
  2. Apes—Juvenile literature. [1. Apes.
  2. Monkeys] I. Title.
  QL737.P9L85   1982   599.8   82-12779
  ISBN 0-516-01633-4   AACR2

TABLE OF CONTENTS

One monkey is getting a drink; the other one
is looking for peanuts.

MONKEYS AND APES

Have you ever watched monkeys and apes? Sometimes they act like people. They play and have fun. They can use their hands the way people do. They peel bananas, pick up food, and play ball.

Proboscis monkey. The word proboscis (pro • BOH • sis) is used to describe a very long or big nose, such as an elephant's trunk.

OLD WORLD MONKEYS

Today monkeys who live in Africa and Asia are called Old World monkeys. Some of them have tails, but some do not. All Old World monkeys have nostrils very close together.

Old World monkeys have names like colobus, langur, baboon, and guenon. They

Baboon

are bigger and stronger
than New World monkeys.
Some Old World
monkeys live in trees.
Others live on the ground.

NEW WORLD MONKEYS

The monkeys that live in South and Central America are called New World monkeys. Many of these monkeys have long tails. They can use their tails like a hand. The nostrils of New World monkeys are very far apart.

New World monkeys are small. The biggest weigh

Right: Woolly monkey
Below right: Cottontopped
marmoset
Below left: Spider
monkey

only about 15 to 20 pounds. All New World monkeys live in trees.

If you hear about a spider, a capuchin, a woolly, a howler, or a night monkey, you will know they are New World monkeys.

All monkeys are primates.

Chimpanzees

APES

Apes are primates without tails. Apes are smarter than monkeys. The large ones are the great apes. Chimpanzees, orangutans, and gorillas are great apes.

Chimpanzees are very active. They like to play.

The orangutans and gorillas are very quiet. They do not move around very much. They are large and heavy.

Gorillas look fierce, but they are not fierce. They are called "the gentle giants of Africa." Sometimes male gorillas grow as tall as six feet and weigh 450 pounds.

Orangutan

Gorilla

White-cheeked gibbon

Gibbons are lesser apes. Gibbons never weigh more than 30 pounds. They live in trees. They use their long arms to swing from tree to tree. Some people call them tree walkers.

Apes live in the Old World. They can be found in Africa and Asia.

HOW MONKEYS LIVE

The night monkeys sleep during the day. They look for food at night. Their bright eyes have white patches above them. They show up in the dark forests. A mother, father, and baby usually travel together. The father takes care of the baby except at feeding time.

Owl monkey
at night

Sometimes the night monkeys are called owl monkeys.

The howler monkeys are the largest of the New World monkeys.

Howler monkeys have "howling times." A male monkey begins making a noise. Then all the others who are around join in. They begin about five o'clock in the morning and howl for about an hour. Other troops of howler monkeys answer them.

Red Howler monkeys

This helps the monkeys stay out of each other's way while looking for food. The tails of these monkeys have prints on the underside just like fingerprints. Their tails are very strong.

Above: Squirrel
monkey
Right: Black-handed
spider monkey

22

The squirrel monkeys are tiny. They weigh only two or three pounds. Their tails cannot be used for swinging in the trees.

Spider monkeys spend most of their time up in the trees. They are big monkeys. Their tails are longer than their bodies. Some of them weigh 15 pounds.

The spider monkeys are fast. They almost seem to fly across the tops of the trees. Their tails are strong. Their tails can hold all of their weight. If they are scared, they break off branches and throw them. They can also make barking noises.

The woolly monkeys have short thick fur on their heads. That is how they got their name. They

South American
woolly monkey

hunt on the ground and in the trees. They can walk on two legs if they use their arms to keep their balance. Sometimes they sit down and use their strong tails to hold them up.

Only the howler monkeys are larger than the woollies.

The capuchin monkeys spend a lot of time on the ground. They are smart. They can use sticks to get food they can't reach. They open nuts by hitting them against something hard. The capuchin monkeys are the organ-grinders' monkeys. They are small, easy to train, and can put on a good show.

Capuchin

27

The baboons are able to live on the ground or in the trees. Many of them are fierce. They will fight other animals.

Some monkeys travel in groups. These groups are called troops. A troop has a male monkey as a leader. The troop always includes females and their babies. There could be other males in the group, too.

Baboons

They live and travel
together to look for food.
They eat insects, leaves,
small birds, birds' eggs,
and fruit. When they find
plenty of food they stay
awhile.

HOW APES LIVE

Chimpanzees like to live in large groups of 70 or 80. They form small groups or troops to look for food.

Gorillas live in troops. They like to be together. A big male is the leader. He is always one of the oldest males.

Male, lowland gorilla

Monkeys and apes that live on the ground need a strong leader. The leader works hard to keep his troop safe.

The troop travels through the forest looking for food. They spend six or eight hours a day looking for food and eating it.

They eat leaves, insects, eggs, and vines. Some apes even eat meat. But gorillas and orangutans

Chimpanzee

usually eat vegetables and fruits.

If anything scares a gorilla troop, the leader puts on a show. He growls and hoots. Then he cups his hand and beats his chest. It makes a loud empty sound.

After making these sounds for awhile the leader hits the ground to make even more noise. Then he runs through the forest and slaps at the bushes. He jumps up and down. He wants to scare away the enemy, not fight.

The other males help the leader make noises. Even the baby apes beat on their chests and scream. They also slap their little bellies or hit another ape. They want to help save the troop.

Five-month-old gorilla

Baby orangutan

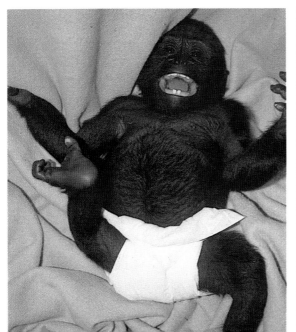

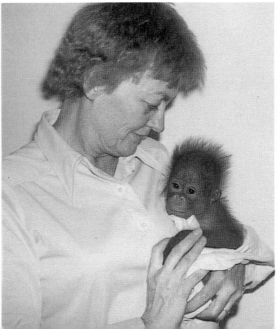

BABY MONKEYS AND APES

Monkeys and apes are good parents. They help their babies grow up.

The mother monkeys and apes nurse their babies. The babies drink their mothers' milk.

Above: Capuchin monkeys and baby
Left: Pigmy chimpanzee and baby

The mothers take very good care of their babies. They keep them warm and safe. When the babies are tiny, they stay with their parents all the time.

The young have many things to learn. They need to know which plants are good to eat and how to find water. They must learn their place in the troop. They must know what the sounds made by the grown-ups mean. Some sounds tell them that danger is near. If they know these sounds, it can save them from getting hurt. They learn all these things from their mothers.

Left: Golden lion marmoset
Above: South American titi monkey

SOME THINGS
TO REMEMBER

New World monkeys are smaller than Old World monkeys. Apes are the largest and strongest of all.

Long-tailed
macaque

New World monkeys
have nostrils that are far
apart and face sideways.

Old World monkeys have
nostrils that are close
together. They face
downward and outward.

New World monkeys cannot use their thumbs to pick up things.

Old World monkeys have thumbs that can be used opposite another finger to pick things up. This is called "opposable."

Can you see the thumb on this monkey?

New World monkeys often have strong tails that can wrap around things. They are prehensile tails.

Old World monkeys never have prehensile tails.

Apes have no tails.

New World monkeys live in trees. They are usually smaller than Old World monkeys.

There are many more interesting and exciting

Rhesus monkey

things to find out about
monkeys and apes. There
is always something new
to learn. Many people
study them. They go to the
forests where the monkeys
and apes live. They watch
them to find out about

Siamangs are the largest gibbons.

them. You can read more books about the things monkeys and apes do. You can go to the zoo to watch them.

When someone tells you that you are "monkeying around," you will know that they mean you are having fun!

WORDS YOU SHOULD KNOW

balance(BAL • ence) — to be in a steady position

fierce(FEERSS) — dangerous

nostril(NAHSS • trill) — one of the outer openings of the nose

nurse(NERSE) — to feed a young animal at a milk gland on the mother animal

opposable thumb(op • OZE • uh • bil) — a thumb that can be used with another finger to hold things

prehensile tail(pree • HEN • sil) — a part of an animal's body that can be wrapped around an object

primate(PRY • mait) — a mammal animal group that includes human beings, monkeys, and apes

props(PROPSS) — something used to keep another thing in position; a support

sac(SACK) — a baglike structure hanging from an animal's body

INDEX

About the Author:

Mrs. Lumley is a nationally known reading specialist and author of numerous books and articles on reading and its teaching. Her experience includes teaching at all levels from elementary through university classes, and director of the Reading Center for the Washington, D.C. Public Schools. Mrs. Lumley is a member of the board of directors of Reading is Fundamental (RIF). She is also a Trustee of the Williamsport (Pa.) Area Community College and is an active participant in leading professional associations.